Symbiosis

A Poetry Conversation

by

Patricia M Osborne and Brian McManus

First published 2022 by The Hedgehog Poetry Press,

5 Coppack House, Churchill Avenue, Clevedon. BS21 6QW

www.hedgehogpress.co.uk

ISBN: 978-1-913499-94-5

INTRODUCTION

Poetry Conversation as a concept is a relatively new means of interpreting poetry, where poets collaborate to respond to each other's work within a pre-defined theme, the general idea being that the whole is greater than the sum of its parts.

The umbrella theme of *Symbiosis* interprets the natural world with a bit of a twist. Poems incorporate Geopoetics, Intellectual Nomadism, Shamanism, the Underworld, engaging, not only with each other as poets, but with Earth and the Cosmos.

Along the way Patricia and Brian touch on ancient civilisations, meditative passages, the pandemic, light amongst the darkness. Their collective journey, and imperative need to move away from the carnage of the modern world to a new physical and mental architecture, offers the opportunity to shake themselves free of inertia, building a symbiotic interdependency as soldiers of unity in a new, revived world.

This volume of poetry is dedicated to all those who work tirelessly to improve and support our challenging modern world, without the recognition they so richly deserve.

Contents

Introduction.. 3
The Intellectual Nomad 7
King of the Forest... 8
3.14... 9
Sacred Messenger.. 10
Koori... 11
River Styx.. 12
Symbiosis.. 13
Bridge with a View.. 14
Partnership 15
Earth's Twin 16
The Hermit Monk and the Scholar Gypsy................ 17
Status Quo... 18
Poiesis... 19
Renascence.. 20
Soldiers in Unity... 21
Rejuvenation... 22

Acknowledgements.. 25
Patricia M Osborne 26
Brian McManus... 26

The dialogue begins with 'The Intellectual Nomad' by Brian McManus then continues alternately.

THE INTELLECTUAL NOMAD

Yes, perhaps.
Primarily mindscape,
rather than landscape.
Esoterica remains cogent,
clear, decisive.

Journeys of place
as relevant, bounteous,
profound through the psyche
as physically peregrinating
the molten sea.

Our joy we hold manifest
in the walking softly
upon our great earth.
Seeing elevated beyond looking.
Travelling in the sublime

sensation of consciousness.
Disavowing the subliminal.
Building our inviolable bond
with blue-grey rocks, oceans,
the singing of the cosmos.

Abjuring artifice and pretence,
eradicating dualism, rationalism.
Unravelling the semiology,
recognising the elegant simplicity of life.
Delivering our great obligations, *pergere ad id.*

Executing the grounding of our own unified contribution.
We hug the Earth, put our arms around the Cosmos.
Transition towards a more transpersonal self.
Make that self and the world we inhabit worth being.
Deny the deceit and the incongruous construct of time.

KING OF THE FOREST

Nature's heartbeat pounds
as seedlings spring up in soil
around the majestic oak.

I wrap my arms around
the tree's wide girth,
place an ear to its bark.

My pulse pumps in tune
to the gurgle of the oak's rhythm.

I kneel under its canopy,
look up as the sky burns fire,

close my eyes,
move into deep meditation.

My spirit roams past druids
in white robes, chanting
as they perform a solstice ritual.

The sun god shines down.

3.14

Standing sentinel. Upright infinity.
Stretches, caresses the fiery sky
as it acknowledges, welcomes the pantheon.
Softly, murmurs an invocation,
an eternal language of synergy,
of cosmic love.

We recognise our sadly depleted earth.
Our joy, and our burden.
Fundamental ground of being.
Comfortably numb no longer,
we shake ourselves free
of heaviness, dullness and inertia.

Turn towards a withdrawal
from the modern dilemma.
Instead, the forging of a consociation.
Life groups. Immediacy of purpose,
argot of tranquillity, movement.
The circumference becomes our norm.

SACRED MESSENGER

Sensitive to Nature,
my spirit free,
I shapeshift –

twist and turn,
become round of girth,
my head shrinks,
grows a pointed bill

that grips a sprig
of olive vine.

In slow motion, I spread
my new long white wings,
lift into amber skies, flutter
across the sea with Geddes'
message for humanity.

KOORI

Transformed, I answer the call.
I carry a message of love, hope and peace.
My journey, blessed by our father of the skies,
reposed in his great golden house
on the 16th floor of the heavens,
as the sun, moon and stars
pay homage at his feet. I depart.

I drift past *Temir Taixa*, the great mountain
of iron. Vaunted pilgrims ascend the rockface.
Yer Messi, the cavernous jaws of the world,
beckon provocatively. Souls to be delivered,
an audience awaits with the King of the Dead,
Lord of the Underworld.
I extend my tensile wings, and soar.

Gnostic spirits align with the floating world,
clear of the domain of Scylla and Charybdis,
the pellucid burning of the paleotechnic,
the vexatious drama of the necrologist.
By the fruits of the soil we live, breathe
with the blue-grey oceans and rocks.
My journey complete, my message delivered.

I turn to face you. Will you too answer the call?

RIVER STYX

In my changeling white feathered form,
I soar over blue waters of Acheron, slip
through the crack and past the hidden gates of Hell.

Corpse bones linger as I glide across
grey lily pastures in the shadowy kingdom.

Charon removes an obol
from the noble soul's mouth,
loads him into the black skiff.
I hover in darkness.

His fiery eyes glow like lanterns as he steers
the boat with a pole through murky waters.

My presence undetected, I fly towards the exit,
reach the cleft at Cape Matapan
and escape from Hades.

SYMBIOSIS

A black water.
A festering conduit.
Boiling with lust, venom.
Seething necrophagist.

Pacified only when birthing
upon the earth, under the sun.
Tamed by the moon, the tides.
Guided by the stars.

Descending from glaciers,
running with ice floes.
Mothered by our natural world.
A loving, imperative symbiosis.

BRIDGE WITH A VIEW

I lean over a trestle footbridge,
watch the winding river as it slows
and flows into a heart-shaped lake.

A bumblebee flits past, darts
to a pendulous branch, sips
sweet nectar from willow's
silken, flaxen bloom.

Mayflies swarm towards hawthorn
along sunlight's golden rays –
translucent, spotted wings glisten.

A turquoise damselfly glides
over limpid ripples, lands
on a pink lily pad, folds her wings.

Sundown blazing russet-red,
I take a deep breath, smile
and stroll home.

PARTNERSHIP

The river sparkles, weaves its way
through our natural world.
Irrigates, nourishes, replenishes,
flushes out decay, dislocation.

We look out from our trestle bridge,
ponder on the gifts we enjoy.
Doff our caps in testament
to our great fortune.
Renounce trauma, repudiate pain,
build back safer, stronger, smarter.

What we see around us from our trestle bridge
is bountiful, munificent, lustrous life.
We have tasted life's underside,
visited its underbelly,
faced-down its threats, its terrors,
refuted its modality, rebutted its tyrannies.

Our minds are clear,
our course is set,
we reaffirm our partnership
with our earth - our cosmos.

EARTH'S TWIN

Drawn to the towering inferno ahead,
I trail along the gravel footpath,
until I reach burnished gold stems
fanning like flames.

With a back canvas of dark conifers,
cornus midwinter fire waves in glory

and baby moon boasts multi-headed
yellow blooms. I inhale the strong scent,

rest on the park bench
and close my eyes.

When I wake to darkness
morning star offers me light.

THE HERMIT MONK AND THE SCHOLAR GYPSY

The ancient kingdom,
crown of the world,
resting place of the circumpolar.

Adrift on the seaboard,
without anchor in a stylised world,
warriors in the dialectic of eros and logos.

Up the back, across the moors,
towards the ocean,
screened by dark conifers.

Cross-legged,
in a field of golden daffodils,
sit the hermit monk, the scholar gypsy.

One orthodox, eclectic,
the other travelling,
towards the circumference.

The status quo,
or embracing the cosmos.

STATUS QUO

An announcement shakes the nation
but Nature stays the same.

Bluetits trill as they flit from sycamore to oak,
daffodils shoot up, bob their golden heads
while pink blossom adorns the cherry tree.

I position my patterned mask,
ruby flowers one side,
the reverse plain maroon.

My blue eyes widen,
small nose and mouth hidden,
protecting others as I breathe.

I follow the marked yellow spots
on the ground while in a queue.

Chat small talk to the woman in front
as I wait with trepidation

       for a jab in my arm,

hoping this vaccination will save our world,
allow me to hug my loved ones,
feel normal again,
travel to the seaside and beyond.

I'm ready to wave farewell to this status quo
and embrace life – the cosmos.

POIESIS

Nightmare visions recede as jabs fulfil their purpose.
Oaks continue to gurgle, stretch, reach for fiery skies.
Mayflies, damselflies still swarm, glide. Bluetits trill
as baby moons smile, dip their heads, nod in affirmation.

The Hermit Monk, banished, wheedles his spurious wares
to well-heeled cognoscenti on barren but inscribed ground.
The Scholar Gypsy treads the seaboard, softly, a peripatetic
nomad at ease travelling in Pelagian space along the Bird Path,

baptised by the foaming spittle of pulsing primordial rhythms
washing the naked shore. Acknowledging the gulls, rosy gulls.
Defining, clarifying the ethos and language of an elemental,
transpersonal reality rescued from a frothing sea of Samsara.

The journey continues. The road is long, difficult, arduous,
and for many of us, most of us, the journey will never end.
The journey is however *poiesis,* a wing beat in a larger space,
a deconditioning, a repositioning, a responsibility, an obligation.

Until then, and until the next time,
we can travel to the seaside,
and beyond.

RENASCENCE

I take your hand as we step
        on to the shore,
slip off my sandals,
          wade in to paddle.

Scooping water into my palms,
        I splash your face,
cooling your skin from the heat.

I brush your lips with mine,
taste the salt in your kiss.
Our bodies cling as we inhale
this long-awaited moment.

A wave swells and roars,
         rolling closer,

laughing,   we dash away
        from the shore,
tread across golden sands,

sit on a bank in the dunes,
pour from a flask
and sip hot coffee.

As an amber sun sinks into the sea,
we welcome this new world.

SOLDIERS IN UNITY

A copse of oak, dressed in birch,
one august, noble, dominant,
bestriding our diseased world.
The other, subservient, belittled,
a simple tool, crude functionary.

Our world lost,
a tangled upheaval,
need for coppicing.

Fresh roots,
regrowth,
redrawn cartography.

Oak and birch brush hand-in-hand
under splashed blue-grey.

REJUVENATION

I stand under the patriarch's canopy
where high in the shade a robin chirps
his melodic refrain.

Hugging the oak's wide girth, I imagine

the Green Man
racing towards Flora
to take as his May Queen

in symbiosis
to fertilise earth
and create new life.

As I stroll home the sun transforms
the sky's cerulean blue to radiant red.

I smile at our promised revived world.

ACKNOWLEDGEMENTS

Many thanks to Ronnie of Reach Magazine (Indigo Dreams Publishing) in which the following poem was previously published:

Bridge with a view (2021).

Special thanks to Maureen Cullen, Sheena Bradley, Corinne Lawrence, Francesca Hunt and Suzi Bamblett, for their continued support and valuable feedback.

Patricia M Osborne and Brian McManus would like to thank Mark Davidson at The Hedgehog Poetry Press for offering this publishing opportunity and being such an awesome editor to work with.

PATRICIA M OSBORNE

Patricia M Osborne is married with grown-up children and grandchildren. Although Liverpudlian born she now lives in West Sussex. In 2019 she graduated with an MA in Creative Writing (University of Brighton).

Patricia is a published novelist, poet and short fiction writer. She has been published in various literary magazines and anthologies. Previous poetry pamphlets published by The Hedgehog Poetry Press in 2020 and 2021 are *Taxus Baccata, The Montefiore Bride* and *Sherry & Sparkly.*

Patricia has a successful blog at Whitewingsbooks.com featuring other writers. When she isn't working on her own writing, she enjoys sharing her knowledge, acting as a mentor to fellow writers.

BRIAN MCMANUS

Brian McManus lives on the outskirts of Glasgow. He is happily married with grown-up children and grandchildren.

Brian comes from a long working background in public service and operational management. Having now stepped away from the world of work he spends his time pursuing his research interests to support his examination of our rapidly changing world through the lens of poetry and essays.

Previous pamphlets published by The Hedgehog Poetry Press in 2020 and 2021 are *Liar Liar* and *Solastalgia.*

Lightning Source UK Ltd.
Milton Keynes UK
UKHW010652090223
416681UK00007B/1967